POEMS FOR THE LOST

By Terry Kang

Edited by
Amanda Coffin
https://www.fiverr.com/stylusink

Illustrations by
Maurizia Nonnis
https://www.fiverr.com/maurapascal

Formatted for print and screen by
Lyubomyr Yatsyk
https://www.fiverr.com/lyubomyr

TABLE OF CONTENTS

Introduction 1

I. LOSS 5

At This Stage 6

The Day I Knew 7

Lost 10

Let's Go to Hollywood! 12

Tradition 13

The Other Guy 15

Social Media 16

All Working Parts 18

Cursed 20

Honeydew 21

The End 22

II. SEARCH 23

Crack 24

Could've Been 25

Always 27

Everything About You 29

New Year's Eve...30

Nirvana 32

Gatsby..33

I Wonder What the Fortune Teller Will Say...................36

My Muse...37

In the Other Room...39

Don't Tell Me 41

Priorities..42

Modern Romance..43

I'll Never Know...44

Animal Planet...45

What I Want..46

So Eager 47

Clarity 48

And Then the Moment Was Gone 49

Burning Embers 51

All In..52

Then and Now 54

Mirage..56

III. FURY 57

Promise 58

Extremes...59

Cancer..60

Thumb 61

Mad 62

Seafood and Wine 63

The Closer I Get to You 64

Honesty 66

I Can't Decide 67

Yet Again 68

Schoolyard Hero 69

Talents 72

No One 73

I Can't Compete 75

Bitch 76

Epiphany 77

No 78

You Say 79

IV. ADMISSION 81

Admission 82

A Lot of Thinking 83

Awakening 87

Choices 89

What If? 90

On a Desert Island 91

Waste Bin 92

Dad Bod..93

Omega 94

Elon Musk..95

Replicas 96

On/Off...97

Allowances...98

Broken Pieces 99

Dark Cloud 100

The Knight..101

Known 103

With or Without You.......................................104

Push and Pull 106

Honesty..107

Mighty Morphin 108

Let Her Go..109

How Much..110

Thank You 111

Mirror 113

Boring 114

Burn...115

My Friend 118

Alignment 120

No Matter 121

V. SORROW 123

Landing 124

Sometimes I Wonder 125

I'm Sorry 126

Love Songs 127

You / Me 128

Radio 129

Depression 130

I Have to Let Go Now 131

No Matter How Far I Go 133

Let Go 135

Her 136

Secrets 137

Nearer to the End! 138

A Time and a Place 141

Desert Road 142

VI. RESOLVE 145

Lost Part 2 146

Trekkies 149

Stay 152

Fear 155

Assent 159

Art of War 160

Baptism by Fire 161

Acceptance 162

My Quotas 163

Don't Ever Forget.. 164

A Good Run.. 166

Man in the Mirror... 169

Abundance 173

The Key 175

Anchors 176

Questions 177

Visualization.. 179

Nara 180

One Path.. 182

Motives 184

I'm Coming.. 185

Sliver 188

Monday Night... 191

The Sum of All Things 192

Icarus... 194

Morning Routine 195

Trudge 196

It's Happening.. 197

Tenri 199

To Do 201

I Am 202

That Was Then, This Is Now 205

A Toast 207

VII. VISION 209

Lesson of Love 210

The Way It's Going to Be 212

Hope 217

Sorry, No 219

Dust in the Wind 221

To All the Dates I've Had Before 223

The Stranger 225

Find You 226

4th of July 228

Somewhere 229

The Hands of Time 232

Traverse 233

The Purple Room 235

When 238

When Part 2 239

About the Author 240

INTRODUCTION

This book isn't for everyone

It's dedicated to all those
Who were left out
Who weren't picked first or second
Or sometimes weren't picked at all

It's meant for those
Who walk home alone
Or don't have a home to go
Or go there, and still feel they have no place to rest their head

This book is for those who thought they knew all about life
Only to realize they didn't know anything at all
For those who have had love taken from them
And for those who took everything out of love until there was
nothing left to take

This book is dedicated
To those who have given their all
And lost it all
And don't know whether to give again

To those who feel everything
But have no one
Or to those who have everything
But it's never enough

This book is for those
Who stand for the truth
Yet stand alone
Once the truth is told

It's for those who hide behind masks
Creators of their own illusions
Because deep inside
They feel that no one will ever love them for who they are

It's for those who don't want to be pitched and sold
Flipped and converted
Because they want to see things for what they are
Not for what others want them to see

This one goes out
To the overly sensitive ones
The nice guys and unwanted girls
The type Bs and sizes over or under

This one goes out to those who were once kids
Who sacrificed days and nights studying for tomorrow
But look around at their lives today
And wonder what it was all for

This is for also for those who were once kids
Who didn't sacrifice anything at all
Except the nights they burned away
And now wonder what it was all for

This is for those who have made it to the mountaintop
And can say with all honesty,
"This was once me.
There are still others out there like me."

I may have experienced more than you
I may have experienced less
But this is me
And this is for you

I. LOSS

AT THIS STAGE

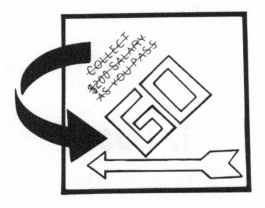

I thought by now
I would've had things figured out
Locked down life's priorities
Achieved my major milestones
And be sippin' on mai tais from Malibu to Macau with you

Instead, here I am
Starting all over

THE DAY I KNEW

Walking in the park
Kids running through fountains
The sun was bright
The air was cool
We were together
And life was good

We held hands
And prayed
I told you that I loved you
You squeezed my hand
And told me
You felt the same way too

Now, after all these years
After all the joys
And all the turmoil
After all the hurt that we've created for ourselves
Against ourselves and against each other
You told me the truth

That day in the park
That spark that ignited us
You didn't take me there to tell me you loved me
You took me there to tell me
You didn't have any feelings for me at all

Thanks, but no thanks
So long and good-bye

Somehow, you just got swept up by the tides of my emotion
And rode the feeling that I had for you
Like a kid riding on a water slide
Enjoying a day at the water park
Swept up
But never swept away from within

Somehow, we built a life together
One house, two kids
Eight years
And all in
Somehow, you made that feeling last
Through all that time

But after all these years
It finally made sense
Why you never reached out to me
Why I could feel your kindness but never your desire
You accepted my advances
Without making any of your own

It makes sense
Why you'd want me to fight so hard for you
But were so easily willing to let me go
I burned the torch so brightly for you
Without ever stopping to realize
You didn't burn for me at all

When you finally told me the truth
My belly was already bloated with contempt
My mind addled with resignation
I knew it was finally time
Time to let you go too

Thanks, but no thanks
So long and good-bye

LOST

Lost in space
I'm lost in space
My ship exploded, and I'm lost in space

It's OK. I'm OK.
The engineers, the administration, God
They did this to me

It would seem
I've somehow changed my native code
With the "If-Only" virus

I'm lost in space
It's so easy
To get lost

But as I float here in the void
I realize blaming others
Doesn't get me any closer to home

It just leaves me with the frustration
Of having no excuses to give
As to why I'm still here

Still lost in space
It's so easy
To stay lost

Because the truth is,
It's not about him or her, it or them
It's me

Just me

The result of all my choices and all my actions
A journey fueled not by courage
But by fears, desires, and deep insecurities

So I reprogrammed myself,
And now I'm up and running
With the It's-All-Up-to-Me code

That's it!
That's the code I need to finally get home!
Geez. Finally.

The only problem is
How the hell do I use it?

LET'S GO TO HOLLYWOOD!

EXT. SUNSET – DAY

Good Guy rides off with Beautiful Girl into the sunset.

FADE OUT**

**Writer's Disclaimer:*
- *Good Guy is really an asshole.*
- *Beautiful Girl is likely to leave Good Guy after the closing credits.*

TRADITION

I always used to see them
Women in my country
Beautiful and subservient
Dutiful to their family
Kind and loyal to their husbands

Chattering happily from the kitchen
Exchanging pleasantries
Serving delicious food
As the kids ran around happily
Like blind and oblivious fools

Everything was neat
But everything was far from perfect
I hated it even then
Because I saw all the pain
Seeping through the corners

So I wanted to pave my own way
Express my own thoughts
Just as I wanted you to express yours
But I didn't know
Never knew it would end like this

Now I see all that remains from the old ways
Happiness and compliance

Even if it's just on the surface
But I'm not the man on the other side
Their faces are unrecognizable
And they give zero fucks about our traditions

And me
I long to be on that other side now
Zero fucks to give either
About truth and authenticity
I'd give anything
For that goddamn façade

THE OTHER GUY

There seems to be some other guy

Whom you look at
When you don't think I'm looking at you

Whom you'd rather be talking about
When you don't want to talk to me

Whom you criticize in your words
While trying to hide the longing in your voice

On good days
I convince myself he's not real

On every other day
He's there
Residing in the spaces between us

He's there when your mind drifts from me
At home
On the phone
Over dinner
In Hawaii

Don't worry
I've always been good at pretending he's not there

SOCIAL MEDIA

Comparing my insides to the outsides of others
Is not a good way to spend an evening
Beautiful homes with crackling fireplaces
Pearly white teeth against sunset backdrops
Delicious meals in exotic locales
Happy, whole families
I should know better than to do this to myself

Can I be happy for you without feeling a loss for myself?
To give you a heart or a thumbs-up coupled with some witty
comment
While refraining from saying, "Way to humblebrag, you
arrogant fuck."
To applaud your adventures in life
While being at peace with the lack in mine?

I won't ask for anything authentic or personal
Let's spare ourselves the embarrassment

I see pictures of us when we were young
And ask myself how everything went wrong
How did it end so quickly?
Why didn't we end up in the house with the white picket fence?
What happened to all those Sears family portraits
That we were going to make into Christmas cards
For all our friends to see?

How did I get to this age
With such tired legs and so little to show?
Other than my children,
Did I just waste the last twenty years of my life?
Burrowing through the rabbit hole into the lives of others
Only makes me fall deeper into the never-ending questions of mine
I should know better than to do this to myself

I need to regroup and refocus
Rather than scrolling through the posts of your delightful lunch and family vacation
I need to go back to building something for myself
Anything to prevent me from looking back in another twenty years
And asking myself "why not?" and "how come?"
And once I do, once I get there…

Maybe then I'll post a picture or two

ALL WORKING PARTS

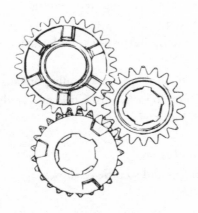

I wonder what it's like
To have all working parts,
Asks the handicapped person
Who was never able to run

I wonder what it's like
To grow up with all working parts,
Asks the child in a broken home
Never built from a blueprint of love

I don't know what I'm missing
But I know something's not there,
Says the one living in the world
With chemicals missing in his brain

I wonder if those who have all working parts
Are thinking about how good they've got it
Or if they just do what comes naturally
And live life without care

I wonder if there's anyone out there
Who actually has all working parts
Or if we're all just broken inside
Somehow and in some way

Still, some are better off than others
This I know for a fact
Thanks God, you're the best
Why are you in control again?

CURSED

It's a curse
To still want you this much

HONEYDEW

Bacon
Cabbage
Milk
No sex

THE END

Twenty years with God
Ten years with you

You left me
I left Him

Nothing makes sense anymore
So let's just have some fun

II. SEARCH

CRACK

They say
Spend time alone
Know thyself
Happiness comes from the inside

I say
Got it
Sure thing
Yeah yeah yeah

Because
Nothing compares
To being wanted
By someone you want

That pure adrenaline rush

COULD'VE BEEN

Mutual likes
Instant rush
Followed by a pretty nifty question
About your epic search for perfect noodles
You LOL'd and replied
We chatted
More laughter
It was good
It could've just been in my imagination
But it seemed so good

When we first met
Your smile was so bright
Your spirit so positive and pure
We talked while eating our favorite food

I felt comfortable around you
You weren't stunningly beautiful
But there was something stunningly beautiful about you

You told me your story
And I told you mine
Same age
Similarities in life
Familiar goals
You were so positive
Everything was so positive
Things were looking so bright

We met again
And again
Each time we were getting closer
Carnival
More texts
Holding hands in the dark
Sharing more of each other

And then you were gone
A phone call
A clean and direct cut
No connection, you said
Thank you for your honesty, I said
And I never saw you again

I thought we had something good
But it could've just been in my imagination
Evidently it was

ALWAYS

I just want to be still
With you next to me
Not thinking of what's next
Or what I should
Or shouldn't be doing

We could be cooking in my apartment
And I wouldn't be worrying
That it's not a house along the sun-drenched coast
Because for now
It's home for us

We could be cutting out pictures
Making collages of our dreams
Talking about what we'll accomplish
Because even at our age
There is so much to look forward to

But mostly we'd be talking
Eating and drinking
Just having fun in each other's company
We enjoy so much
Being in each other's company

And I wouldn't want this night to end
Even though we know

There will be so many more like it
Because there'll never be another night exactly like tonight
With just you and me

I think of these days as good ones
As I sit alone and write like this

EVERYTHING ABOUT YOU

I love everything about you
Which is not very much, I know
I want to love everything about you
Even the things you don't want me to see

I want to love you on your good days
But also on your bad days
And most especially on your worst days
The days when you might feel all alone

I love all the good parts that I see
Your beauty, your emotional depth,
Your eyes, the smell of your hair
Your dreams, your hopes, your kind heart

I want to love all the parts that I don't see
The way you might act if you don't get your way
The way you might feel when you think back on your past
The way you might get mad
Or sad
When a day or life in general seems particularly hard

I want to love everything about you
All the good parts
But also the bad parts
Especially the bad parts
Because that's what love is

NEW YEAR'S EVE

When the countdown came
We celebrated with champagne and roses
Chocolate and silk sheets
And a room with a view

What I saw
Was you saying yes to spend this day—this particular day—
with me
You, wearing your beautiful red dress, just like you promised
And you, taking my flowers home the next morning

What I chose not to see
Was you pulling away on 3-2-1
While others danced and kissed the night away in celebration
You, texting away on your phone

You, pulling away
Keeping your distance

I thought that you just had your walls
Maybe you had been hurt in the past
I was so intent
On being the one who could change that

But the closer to you I try to get
The lonelier I become

I guess I could press harder
Overwhelm you with my devotion
But any walls I break would only come back up
If you never broke them down for yourself

While making something out of nothing
Is something I'm comically good at
Maybe I just need to get better
At being honest with myself

You warned me that I would be hurt
But I chose to take my chances
This was my choice to go as far as I did
And now it's my choice to go no further

NIRVANA

You told me once
That if you truly love someone
You should simply be happy for them
Happy that they are well in life
Happy they are free from hurt

But I like you
So much that it hurts
And I wish I could be happy
Happy simply to have known you
Happy simply for the time we had together

But I'm not

One day I hope to be at peace
Free from desire and passion
Free from longing
Free from hope
And to be one with peace

I hope to have
What the Buddhist monks
You once strived to be
Have found for themselves
Until then…

This is what I have

GATSBY

He leaned over from his terrace
And looked down to his expansive courtyard
Where his party was in full swing

He panned through the countless faces
And sifted through all the nonsense
To extract the only thing that mattered

I ask myself what must have been going through his mind
As I look down at my phone
Where your photos are scattered all about

Did he feel the ultimate confidence?
The sweet satisfaction of knowing
The success, the wealth, everything he worked for...

Were finally his?

He could throw these lavish parties now
Even though there was nobody he cared about
And nobody was there who cared about him

He could do this now
He could do anything now
He could be anyone now

For her

All the pushing and all the striving
Just to be the guy who could give her
Everything he thought she needed

But in the end, it wasn't enough, was it?
All the money, all the effort, all the hopes
Amounted to nothing

He took the fall
Despite working unceasingly
To impress her

Maybe through it all, deep down
Maybe he always knew
She would never be his

She would always want the other guy

He of the philandering ways
The bad boy
The low-down, no-good piece of shit

In the end
It would be someone else
It would be anyone else

Still... he thought....
It was worth a shot

Maybe I'll end up like him too
Trying to build a kingdom
Just to get your attention

Giving you everything that I think you need
Giving up everything
Just to impress you

Parties aren't bad
Money is just another goal
Friends can be won

Maybe I'll end up like him too
Fighting alone
Dying alone

Still... I think to myself...
It's worth a shot

I WONDER WHAT THE FORTUNE TELLER WILL SAY

You said you liked me more than him
But I don't know what that means
When you don't like him at all

You said you were going to ask the fortune teller about me
What if she says something good?
Will you open your heart to me?

What if she says something bad?
Will you write me off as a curse?
And let me go forever?

I wonder what the fortune teller will say
My fate to be decided by another
But I guess that's what love is

MY MUSE

Since I've met you
I write more than I ever have
Dream higher than I should ever dare
And burn brighter than I can sometimes bear

If I'm honest with you
You're not the first one that made me feel this way
If you're honest with me
You know I won't be the last one that feels this way about you
But somewhere down the middle
We can have something good

There will be a day soon
When money won't be a thing for me
When fame will be something to avoid rather than something
to pursue
When things will be better… easier…
When I will no longer have to take on the world
Because I will have taken over the world

I want you to come on that journey with me
We can do this together
You can help me fly to the sun
Without burning my wings
I can help you reach the top of the pyramid
That you so earnestly seek

But if your aim is to be a femme fatale
I'll hand the helm to someone else
And let them crash on their own ship
Die on their own time
My goal is to live life to the fullest
Not to be shipwrecked and lost at sea

I can only hold on to my hope of you for so long
Before I continue my journey alone
Perhaps that's what you prefer
Perhaps that's what was meant to be
But that's not what I want

If you chose me now
Even when we're old and grey
I'd still want to burn for you
Still ask you to dance every New Year's Eve
Still want to peel away the layers of love and lust
And still say you were more beautiful than the coastline, the
sunrise, and the sunset

But I won't wait forever

IN THE OTHER ROOM

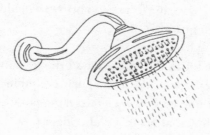

I hear her taking a shower
As I'm in the bed waiting
I had planned for this so meticulously
Yet all I can think about is you

It's obvious there is no love here
Just a matter of mutual convenience
But it's amazing how different she is from you
Responsive
Attentive
Happy to hear from me
Everything I want
And everything you're not

But it's not her I'm thinking about now, is it?
Even as I hear the shower drips subside

I want something with someone that will never be
And this here tonight
This is not what I want

But if I had you
If I really had you
There would always the fear of tomorrow, wouldn't there?
Can I make you happy?
Can I keep you happy?
Can I provide for you in all the ways I think you want?
Would you really want me if you knew everything about me?
Suddenly wanting you never seemed more pointless
Almost as pointless as being with her right now

But maybe that's just life

I hope one day I can be brave and admit this much to her
And I can tell her none of this needs to happen

By that's not going to happen tonight

DON'T TELL ME

Don't tell me all the things I'm not
I already do that very well

Tell me all the good things that I don't see
And all the things I can be

Because that's what I already see in you

PRIORITIES

I just spent my whole paycheck on our last three dates
But told the clerk
That I didn't want to spend ten cents on a grocery bag

MODERN ROMANCE

The truth is
No matter who we are on the inside
We've already made up our minds
The moment we saw each other's pictures on our profile pages

I'LL NEVER KNOW

As I was putting my bags in the car
I realized I had forgotten my ID card

Was it because I was high
That I had forgotten to bring it?

Or was it the reason
I remembered that I had forgotten it in the first place?

ANIMAL PLANET

After spending half my paycheck and all my week
Preparing for our perfect night
I asked you the next morning if you wanted to spend the day
with me
But you preferred
Staying home alone
And watching Animal Planet

WHAT I WANT

What I want
Is to be here
In this moment
With you

Thinking of nothing else but you
And knowing you're thinking of nothing else but me

Even if it's just one moment
It will be a perfect moment

Maybe that's too little to ask of me
Maybe that's too much to ask of you

SO EAGER

I see you
Sitting down at the other end of the restaurant
Dressed so casually in that new blouse that must have taken
you hours to pick
Leaning forward on the table
Eyes bright, smile wide
So eager to please that disinterested guy sitting across from you

I think that is so hilarious

Because you remind me of myself
If I were with you
And you were him

CLARITY

I've written your college papers throughout the night
Taken the red-eye across the world
Reserved your favorite restaurants
And helped you get back your lost gold

So why can't you take the day off for me?

AND THEN THE MOMENT WAS GONE

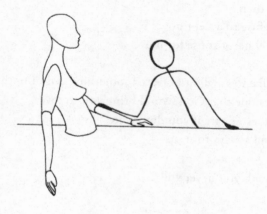

I wanted the moment to last
Tomorrow to never arrive

I prayed the song that we danced to
Would loop lovingly without end

I hoped the sun that would wake us
Would never rear its ugly head

But in bed where we lay
You, rigid to me like stone
Me, entwined with you like rope
I also wished...

That you'd come to life

I gave you my best that night
I gave you my very best

But when tomorrow becomes today
I'll know then
What I refuse to accept now
That you'll never rouse for me

Perhaps like Pygmalion I created something out of nothing
With the hope that God would bring you to love
But He doesn't care if you don't care
Reality will always turn up

Even though you never will

BURNING EMBERS

I stopped reaching out to you
When you made it clear
You'd never reach out to me
But someone forgot to tell you

To put out the fire you left behind

I'm left to snuff out the coals
Sweating alone in my lodge
While you've left hanging
A picture of our night on your profile page

ALL IN

Sometimes I just detonate the bank
And go all in
Or give some excuse why this transaction is different

In the end
It's all the same

Some decisions are obviously bad
Some a little less so
Trying too hard to impress a girl to compensate for my
shortcomings
Obviously bad
Inviting one too many guests to my kid's birthday party
A little less so

Whatever the case

I'm here

With nothing to show

THEN AND NOW

It was thirty years ago when I first saw you
It had been fifteen years since I'd seen you
We reconnected just six months ago
And talked about all the things we did as kids

We're older now
But I still feel the same way about you

You came back to me
At a time when everything was in disarray
I was picking up the pieces
And wondering why

Always wondering why

God couldn't tell me
His silence, as always, was deafening

So I stopped searching for his answers
But talking to you again after all these years…

Maybe God had a plan!

Turns out
He doesn't

MIRAGE

I keep seeing you
For who I want you to be

Thinking there's an oasis
When there's no life for me at all

III. FURY

PROMISE

Thank you
For all the slights
All the declines
All the passes
All the left swipes
And the outright disregards

I appreciate
All the sorry but no's
The thanks anyways
The best wishes
The good lucks
And the you'll get there one days

I promise
I will pay you back for all of it in the end

EXTREMES

Don't mistake
My authenticity
And my willingness to care
As a weakness

Because my other option
Is burning you at the stake
Not with hesitation
But with laughter

CANCER

Why do I play your constructive criticism
Over and over in my head
Like a broken record?

You were right
I was wrong
Let's move on

If only I could
But it's still there
Like the pain of a growing tumor

Like a Pick-a-Path Adventure
Play it again, Sam!
Going back to the crossroads of yesterday
To choose any path except the one that led me here

THUMB

God has a funny sense of humor
Just when you think He's letting up
He presses his thumb down
Just a little bit harder

MAD

Don't give me your logic
And all the reasons why I shouldn't...

I'm angry
Because I want to be

If I let go of that
I don't know if I'll have anything left

SEAFOOD AND WINE

I like seafood and wine
Which restaurant are you going to take me?
Where are all the gentlemen?
I need a real man
Is chivalry dead?
Anything but Asian men

Looking for someone who plans
I love spontaneity!
Serious relationships only
I'm attracted to bad boys
You're too nice
Sorry, no

How do I know you're not like every other guy?
What were you saying again?
I thought you made more money
There wasn't any connection
You're a good guy but there's no chemistry

Wait, you have kids?
Dealbreaker

So many words
Here's two from me

Fuck off

THE CLOSER I GET TO YOU

The closer I get to you
The further I get from her

The closer I get to you
The more focused my mind becomes
The more dedicated I am to the game
The more driven I am toward my goals
The leaner my body gets
Stronger and faster
More aware of who I am and
What I have to do to stake my claim

The closer I get to you
The further I get from her
Until it becomes time
To go back and not care
About promises and loyalty
About gentlemanly ways
No calls the next morning
Just simple transactions
Nothing more nothing less

She and I
We're not in this together
We're not on some serendipitous road toward the Hollywood
Dream

I'm doing it alone
Because I'm not what you're looking for
I won't ever be what you're looking for
And you're not what I need

I won't know her when I get there
But I'm going to get to know her when I do
Her and hundreds like her
All products of my imagination and fears
All in it for one thing and one thing only
That's okay
I'll be that same way too

HONESTY

You think because I have kids that it's some kind of problem?
The fact that I'm divorced is some kind of bitter defect you're
forced to swallow?
And because I'm starting over, it means there was something
wrong with me?

Fair enough
To each their own

But I'm not here to pick up your pieces either
You had your fun
Fell in love with all the chiseled cheekbones with callused
hearts
Until it got too late and you realized
You were never their #1
I tried to repair what was destroyed in another
It was a lot of work
And it didn't work
Maybe I'd do it again
Maybe for one I valued enough to invest in again
But you're not that person

I CAN'T DECIDE

I can't decide whom I hate more
You for ignoring me
Or me for jumping at every scrap of attention you give me

YET AGAIN

Ah, you got me again
Caught me in one of your downswings
And dropped me on your way up

This one's on me
Just like the time before that
And the time before that

You have the problems
And I have the solutions to fix them
And that's my problem

SCHOOLYARD HERO

So this is what I need you to do, son
I want you to go out to that playground
Yes, that one with all the bigger kids
Yes, I know they're stronger too
Listen
Stop interrupting
I want you to go there in front of all those kids
And tell them

They're all fucking stupid

What?
No, they're not my kids
What kind of question is that?
You're my son

I have no idea where those kids came from
Other parents, I guess
Not me
They're not my kids
You're my kid. You're my son

So will you do that?
Yeah, just go out there and tell them
No, no, no
Not like that. Don't do it like that
Do it exactly like how I told you
Mad? Yes, of course they're gonna get mad
They'll be super mad!
In fact, they'll be so mad that they'll come right up to you
And want to beat you up

But don't worry
I'll be here the whole time
I'm not gonna leave you. I'll never forsake you
I'll wait until they get close
Super close
And right when they get close enough to touch you,
I'll swoop in and deliver you
I'll run up to the playground
And blast all those mofos that dared step up to you

Will you do that?
OK. But you gotta do it exactly like I said
It creates the narrative
So when I come in and do my thing
I'll look so fucking cool

All the other parents will be in awe
Especially Stacy's mom
She's got it going on
Do that for me, OK?

Because
You're my son
And I'm your dad

TALENTS

I constantly amaze myself
By how much I give to you
While getting absolutely nothing back
It's a talent, really

NO ONE

I asked you for so long
To take away my thorns
To make me stronger
As I worked to be better in heart and spirit
For your means, not my ends

It all seems so foolish now

Heaven forbid
My children depend on me when they're old
Asking me for guidance without fail
Relying on my eternal wisdom for every choice they make
And not following their own path

That would be so fucking foolish

Took me so long to accept
I'm a consequence of my own decisions
A result of my own actions
My successes are all my own
And so are my failures

I'll no longer give you any of it

If you take me out
As you're prone to do to those who give a damn

73

You'll do so without my permission
If you bless me
Then do it

There are only so many sacrifices and tears
That I can make on my knees
Before I realize
My life is best lived on my own two feet

I CAN'T COMPETE

I can walk the earth with all the bravado
But right now
The truth is…
 I can't compete

I don't have a lot of money, a nice home, a nice car
I'm a single parent
Average looking
Average in bed at best

Did I really think… women would want me for my
personality?
My virtues?
Hahahahah
What virtues?

Time to be honest with myself
Take a step back
Redefine myself
The game isn't changing

Redefine myself
And fuck them all

BITCH

Pouting and moaning
You sure do that very well
How about
You shut the fuck up for a change
Keep that mouth shut
And finish your goddamn job?

Do you want to spend the rest of your life
Whining about how things should be easier?

That's for someone else's life
Not mine

EPIPHANY

Took me this long to realize
I need to do this on my own

So essentially,
I'm fucked

NO

I don't think
Love should be this hard

I no longer want it to be

YOU SAY

You say I'm desperate for love
And maybe you're right

Maybe I am

IV. ADMISSION

ADMISSION

We're all lost
Just a matter of when and how you realize it

A LOT OF THINKING

Thanks for meeting me
Do you want to order something?
I know you have a lot of questions
But I thought it best we do this in person

I owe you that much

We've been through a lot
We've been through everything together
But it's time I'm honest with you
It's time I told you the truth

It's over

I've been feeling this way for a while
Longer than I'm willing to admit
I was hoping things would change
Hoping we could make our dreams work

But living the way we have
Continuing on like we have
Making the same mistakes over and over
Let's just admit it

This won't work

We've talked about this before
You kept putting this off
You promised that things would be different
You kept promising that things would be different

But you keep coming up with the same excuses
It's always someone else's fault
Those who don't give you what you want
Those who keep passing you by
The upbringing you didn't have
The time that you lost chasing your God
The shortcomings God has given you
The instability you have in your head
The love who left you
The love you're waiting for
The battles of the Haves and Have Nots

It goes on and on and on

I'm not going to sit here
And watch it all pass away
There may not be tomorrow
So I'm moving on today

I'm doing this without you

I want more than this
I've left you to navigate the ship
And you've left me with nothing
But a ticket to the island of mediocrity

I want to break barriers
I want to live up to my true potential
I want to go beyond my default
I want to go beyond my default

But it's not you, it's me

I let this happen
It was so easy to let this all happen
Never once taking control
Never once taking responsibility

Blaming you for everything

I need to grow up
By leaving myself no excuses
And making tough decisions
Even if that means letting things go

Letting you go

So I'm saying good-bye
I'm sorry for all the bad decisions I helped make
I'm sorry for holding us back
And running on this path for as long as we have

If we're lucky
We'll meet again as changed souls
If we're not
We'll be right back here together again

Good luck, my brother
You were the best friend I ever had
But even best friends need to grow up
Even us

Especially us

AWAKENING

I woke up
After having dreamed of you
You were getting undressed
I had forgotten how beautiful you were
I was looking at women on my phone
I had forgotten how I stupid I can be

I asked
Are you going to Hawaii with me?
I don't know
Do you want to go to Hawaii with me?
The divorce papers are in the mail
Well, you either want to go with me or you don't

But asking you the same thing over and over
Is what got us here in the first place

After all this time
I never realized how alone we were
Having friends but not really
Having kids but no help
Just trying to keep our heads above water
Just trying to swim past the breakers

I reached for you
And then I woke up

After all this time
Thinking I was better off without you
Feeling so little through our parting
It finally dawned on me

None of me is happy

CHOICES

When does a mistake
Become a lifestyle?
When does a lifestyle
Define a life?

I've lost count
Of all the times I've repeated
All the things I promised
I'd never do again

Addicted to love
Crippled from progress
The outward search
To fill an inward need continues

How much time do I have left?
Eventually I'll need to stop
Because I want to love myself more
Than wanting to be loved by you

WHAT IF?

What if I get to the top of the mountain
And find out that there were no evil conspiracies?
No oppressive forces out to get me?
No demons thwarting my every endeavor?

What if I reach the top of the mountain
Just to find out
That the only reason I hadn't gotten here earlier
Was because I was lazy?

ON A DESERT ISLAND

The man was aloof
Didn't reach out
Didn't feel the need to reach out
She wanted his approval so much
He didn't care enough to give it
But with her strength and skills, she showed him her worth
And his heart warmed to her
And she felt accomplished and good

Some people are like this

WASTE BIN

Met with my financial advisor today
To go through my plans for tomorrow
One of the lines at the top of my list
"Save $50,000 for a wedding in 5 years."

"Delete that," I told her
And she dragged it into the waste bin

How quickly we grow up

DAD BOD

I'd rather be fat from eating too much with my kids
From all the dinners I make them
Than be super fit and lost in my own self-conceit

But do you really think I need to lose some weight?

OMEGA

All my hurt
All my fear

I medicate it all
With all the things you hate

And that's why there's always an end to us
And never a real beginning

ELON MUSK

I love how you put on a mask
For all the world to see

Perhaps if I had Elon Musk money
Elon Musk vision
And Elon Musk intelligence
I wouldn't have to wear masks

But then again perhaps Elon Musk
Wears a mask of overly burdensome emotions

REPLICAS

Some look promising
While others aren't worth a second glance
They're all just counterfeits
Facsimiles
Replicas

When I find it I'll know
Got my checklist in hand
But in the end, it won't be complicated
I'll see it and I'll know
When I see it, I'll know

We all just want what's real in the end
(At least I think that's so)
The rest of it is just biding our time
Or building experience points along the way
In the end, we'll know
Everything else was just replicas

ON/OFF

Some people turn on
And some people turn off

Those who turn on
Get so triggered
They won't turn off
Even when the house is going down in flames

Those who turn off
Get so put off
They'll use every reason
To never enter the house at all

ALLOWANCES

I used to give myself so many allowances
A piece of pie
A Netflix binge
A nights of drinks (or five)
A date with a new interest

I wanted it
I needed it
Granting myself the allowance
Was the best form of exercise

Just desserts
Because I deserved it

And what I got in return
Was nothing at all

It's hard to believe I've lived so long
And achieved so little
I'm almost in awe
If it weren't so depressing

A little momentum
Will get noticeable results
To motivate me for the next step

But to get to where I want to go
Requires zero allowances

BROKEN PIECES

Always running around
With hammer and nails
Trying to fix the broken pieces in you
Trying to fix all the broken parts

Because that's what love is

Let me open the door
Let me help you with your essay
Tell me where to pick you up
Whatever I can do to help

Because that's what love is

I've always chased you
Wanted to overwhelm you with affection
Wanted to prove myself with devotion
Because nothing was too much for you

Except that's not what love is

Because there's only one thing broken in this equation
It's the one chasing and chasing
Proving and proving
To someone who is not there

To someone who will never be there

DARK CLOUD

I'd love to be your bright sky
Full of laughter
Joy and bliss
But I want to know the meaning behind your underlying
clouds
The reasons why you say can't get up in the morning

But that's not what you want to talk about
It's never the time; it's never the place

You want laughter and fun
Fast cars and sunset boulevards

I wish I could be like that
And not just for you

THE KNIGHT

A man is raised

To be a knight in shining armor
To march before the dragon
And save the beautiful princess

To be bold and to be strong
To do anything for his beloved
And save her from distress

A man is raised to fight this dragon
No matter what it may cost
To be deemed worthy of her love

A man is not raised

To understand that the dragon
That terrifies his princess
Is not in some hidden castle or faraway land

It's nothing that he can search for
Nor is it something he can destroy
For the dragon that haunts his princess
Is an enemy that she alone must overcome

No, the battle that he must fight
Is the belief that resides within him
That to be worthy of her love
He must fight the battle for her at all

KNOWN

All I want
Is to be known by you

Without you having to see
All the things I'm afraid for you to know

WITH OR WITHOUT YOU

When I have accomplished it all
And sit atop the mountain
Will that be the moment
I'm finally enough for you?

I cheated on Destiny once
To get to Love the first time
But She doesn't forgive
And She doesn't forget

So I was left resenting her
And she… she just left

Maybe I'm just not one to travel as two
Having you sit through all my failures
And having you witness all my moments scraping by
Maybe that's a journey I'm not willing to take

Maybe I'd rather have you just see me at my best
In all its artificial brilliance
And maybe…
Maybe you wouldn't have it any other way

So here I am, groping in the dark,
Reaching for my goals,
Willing myself up this mountain,
And pretending this isn't about you

I don't have a map, only an "X"
Plodding like a blind man mucking through the mire
Not sure I'm getting any closer to where I'm going
Not sure if I'll even know it when I'm there

I don't have a father to light my path
Neither the genes nor the endowment to ease this bitter climb
All I have is a vengeful need for results
And a divine directive to build the next Model T

Oh, great and powerful Father
Spare me a seat on your empty pew
Spare me all your empty promises
While you busy yourself with handing it all to the Jacobs of
this world
But while it might take me forty years
And forty more years after that
Of this I am most definitely sure
I'll make it

That place where I need to go
I'll make it

And when I get there...
Maybe I'll see you there too

Then again
Maybe I won't

PUSH AND PULL

Life is about push and pull
If you're doing too much of one and not the other
You need to re-examine your door

HONESTY

Likely you'll never accept me
But you'll never have to wonder
About where I stand or who I am

MIGHTY MORPHIN

I morph myself
Into something I'm not
To be loved by as many as possible
To avoid rejection as much as I can

Faced with never-ending choices that require their response
I capitulate to appease
A part of me for a part of them
Only to lose myself in the process

I always thought Darwin was right
Survival is for the fittest
Those who adapt to their environment
Are the ones that prevail

But maybe he wasn't

If I can be true to myself
To all the things that I hold dear
Without waving the white flag when times get hard
Authenticity without fear or hesitation

Maybe that's what life is all about

Was this obvious to everyone but me?

LET HER GO

Let her go, bro
After all this time
She ain't picking you
And if she once did
She ain't coming back
And if she does
Do you still want her?

HOW MUCH

How much must you love someone
That even though you want to be with them
You realize they might be better off without you?

That's true love

Hahaha

Dumb motherfucker

That's bullshit

You want someone?
Be everything you can be
And realize if it doesn't work out
You're better off without them

THANK YOU

While bitter and angry
A part of me is relieved
You took the sword and split us
Something I never had the courage to do

I'd like to say you were wrong
And blame you for giving up
But you're right
This wasn't meant to last forever

Aside from all the blame I put on you
And all the anger inside
I was miserable
I probably made you miserable

Sure you had your faults
Quite a few of them I may add
But I had plenty of my own
And despite all my best efforts
I wasn't going to change

Coming home and seeing you
Didn't make me happy
Because it wasn't about you
It was about him

Him. The me that I wanted to see in the mirror
The better me. The more successful me
The me that meant something
The me that I wanted to be

And it was too much to put on you
To try and make you see me that way
How high a burden you had to carry
To make you make me into something I wasn't

So thank you for ending this
For ending our misery for us
Thank you for letting go when I couldn't
And I'm sorry I put you through all this

MIRROR

My children
If you are a reflection of my soul
Than perhaps there is something beautiful about me after all
Because there is nothing in the world more beautiful than you

BORING

I want to live a boring life

Agonizingly monotonous
Eye-rollingly predictable
Unexcitedly formulaic

I want to live an unvarying life

Powerfully consistent
Unwaveringly determined
Remarkably focused

Eliminate all the choices
Take away all the emotions
So I can improve my odds

Just follow the plan

BURN

So many remedies
Made by so many self-proclaimed gurus
All swaying to a sing-along in one big circle-jerk
Low fat, high fat, all meat, no meat
Low intensity, high intensity
No carbs, well-balanced
Nonsense

So many guiding lights
Teaching the way of truth for all
One way, every way
No compromise, all-accepting
One God, many gods
Faith-based, science-proven
Garbage

So many paths to walk
Efficiency setting, goal getting
Outside the box, inner circle
Work smarter, not harder
Inspiration, perspiration
Risk mitigating, risk taking
Bullshit

Allow me a moment
To interject my philosophy

In all its equally esoteric uselessness
The ins and outs
The way I see it
The inner secret
For me

Fire
Is the only way
To light the road
To fuel the path
The antidote to all the quick fixes, silver bullets,
Magical elixirs, golden tickets
Jibber Jabber

If failure is a disease,
Then fire is the surgeon's blade
If losing and waiting,
Excusing and debating
Is the comforting venom
Then fire is the bitter cure

So much folly
I bought into for so long
So much chasing
Other people's truths and doctrine
So much consumption of straight-up toxins
The only answer
Is to burn it all

Now is the time
To work it out, grind it down

Wake up early, stay up late
Pound out the words, distill all the hate
Investing creating producing
Through fire, rampaging endless fire
My sickness' only cure

This is the best thing
The is the only thing
Fire
Set it all ablaze
Burn it all down
To build it all back up

MY FRIEND

My friend

You only have a little time left
Before the moment has passed
And the window has closed

You can no longer afford
To pursue others like a lovelorn teenager
Spending and investing in a bottomless well

You've given your all to others
Now give your all to yourself
Give your all to yourself

If it bleeds, and if it hurts
You know you're on the right path
There are no more excuses

Take a moment
To shut the door completely
Shut the door of romance and love

Because it will not be your refuge
It won't keep you warm in the middle of the night
Or answer the echoes of your heart

Love yourself enough to do this
Love yourself enough to sacrifice it all
Do right by you

My friend,
Do right by you

ALIGNMENT

Until all my intentions
Are followed by my actions
Until all my plans
Are executed with diligence

I'll never find the peace I seek

If I can put aside my comforts
And the need for constant validation
For just a moment
And set my hands to the plow

I can excel in everything I do

NO MATTER

No matter how much I tell you
Throughout the next few poems
That this is no longer about you

It's all a lie

It really is still all about you

V. SORROW

LANDING

Now that you're gone
The words don't come out so easily
The inspiration doesn't flow so freely
Nothing flows off the tap and into the bucket

I stopped reaching out to you
When you made it clear
There was nothing to hold onto
Yet you stoked a fire long lost from within

So I'm left to sweat and conjure coals in this lodge
To chisel rather than to mold
While you've left hanging
A picture of our night on your profile page

SOMETIMES I WONDER

Sometimes I wonder
If I'll ever make it
If I'll ever get to the point where I want to be
And achieve all the things that I want to achieve

And then I wake up
After falling asleep from another Netflix binge
And I'm very confident
That I won't

I'M SORRY

I'm sorry
For making love to you
And thinking of someone else
Or thinking I'd rather be somewhere else

I promise
To never do that again

LOVE SONGS

Different rooms
Different people
But wherever we go
They're all the same songs

I thought they were for us
Songs you would sing only for me
Songs I would sing only for you
But nothing is ever ours

Wherever we go
Whomever we're with
The songs are always the same
At the time, we just happened to be the one listening to each
other's

YOU / ME

I loved you
The moment I saw you
Back then, you were all that I knew

But what I didn't know
Was that you were all I ever wanted to know

How is it you're with me
Wherever I go?
Why do I want to share with you
Whatever I have?

You and he
Me without you
For better or for worse
That's me

RADIO

It took me 41 years to realize
All these love songs from her
Were never about me

DEPRESSION

Two roads diverged in a yellow wood
Neither makes a fucking difference

I HAVE TO LET GO NOW

I thought you just needed time
I felt that even though things were progressing so slowly
They were still progressing
And that meant something
I was so convinced that meant something

In time, you asked to see my kids
And spent New Year's Eve in my arms
You trusted me to take you home
Even though hundreds of others failed to get that far
Surely that meant something

But as I lie here alone
The truth is difficult to avoid

I have this magical ability
To press at every opportunity
To lay you on a bed of roses
And overwhelm you with my love
In return, I need just a sliver of hope

Sometimes it works
Sometimes I make it work
But if there was nothing there from you in the first place
Reality eventually sets in
Reality always sets in

The reality that you'd rather do nothing
Than spend time with me
That you don't return my messages
And never ask to see me
Reality always sets in

Perhaps if I continue to press
I can inch closer to your heart
But I've learned the hard way
If nothing is there to begin with
Then everything can dissolve instantly

NO MATTER HOW FAR I GO

No matter how far I go
I can't shake the feeling
That I'm the same person I used to be
Running on the same emptiness
Restrained by the same insecurities
Set off by the same triggers
Feeling that familiar sense of falling

People don't change
That same lack we had when we were young
Won't be satiated when we grow old
No matter how far we go
How high we climb
We're still the same person in the end

Maybe I can self-validate
Find peace within and make peace without
And be complete within myself
All by myself
Maybe I can get there one day
Then again maybe I won't

Maybe I need your help to get there
To tell me that on my worst day I'm still good enough
And on my best day we can celebrate with sundaes and brownies
Maybe I want you to be here with me
And then again maybe I don't

Regardless, I push on
Now harder and more frequently than ever
To get to where I want to go
Not with you
Not because of you
Not even toward you

I do this for me
For my children
And maybe when I get there
When I look back at how far I've gone and how much I've
done
I hope to realize
That I'm not the same that I once was

LET GO

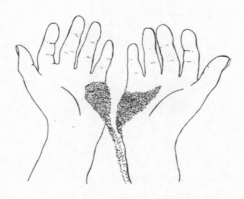

I've learned eventually
To let go

To let go of everything that doesn't want to be held
To let go of the past
To let go of the future
To let go of all the fears and all the hopes
All the love and all the hate
The haves and the have nots
The dos and the don'ts
And all the wants and desires

Whatever is left
Is what is
And whatever has left
Let it be gone

HER

Still
With her I got further than I ever could go on my own
Got a house
Experienced miracles
I felt loved
I felt desired
I felt needed
I felt needed
I felt like I was allowed to lead
Allowed to make decisions to make me feel like a man
I felt like she helped me to be a better man
Even on the days when all I felt like was a boy inside

And I don't understand why that's wasn't enough for me
I don't understand how I could be so selfish and so selfish and
so selfish
And I don't understand why that wasn't enough for me

SECRETS

I'm sorry that after all these years
I didn't tell you my secrets

Next time there will be no secrets
Even if that means I'm all alone

NEARER TO THE END!

My friends
This is the beginning of the end
The nice guys
The sincere ones
The weak ones
We're near the end

Before
We could plead with the lovely ones
We weren't always strong
We weren't always able
We were never the first choice
But we could convince them with a dying oath
We could convince them with our dying oath

And maybe
By past hurts
By limited choices
And confined proximities
We could convince them
By God, how we would need to convince them

But then it happened
With the birth of the Wildfire
We no longer had the advantage of seclusion
The comforts we could provide from the dangers of this world
now means nothing

In a civilized nation, they were safe
And we were doomed

Evolution has taught us
Survival is for the fittest
In an open world
They have access to all the fittest
And that is why, my friends,
We're left out in the dirt

We can improve
We can change
But deep down
There will be a part of us that will remain broken
We're just ones who want to love
Ones who want to be loved
But that, as we've always known, was never enough

That could be the end of our story
Or only the end of our chapter
In the past, we created mountains
Now it's time
To create the largest fucking mountain
The world has ever known

If we build it
We can build it beyond our wildest imaginations
It's not going to be easy
But for us, nothing was ever easy
And the stakes only got higher
But if we build it…
We can define the world

That's why we should stick together
The road is long and hard
And our opposition is unrelenting
But if we keep building ourselves up
So that we continue building on our dreams
We can be great

We can be unstoppable

A TIME AND A PLACE

There is a time
When a man's mind
Must rein in his body

There is a time
When a man's heart
Must speak over his mind

Then
And only then

Will he realize
Just how difficult this journey truly is

DESERT ROAD

I've made so many withdrawals
And enjoyed the ride while it lasted
But I'm maxed out and overdrawn
And find myself, once again, deep in the red in regret

The morning after is bleak
Driving through the desert of broken promises
But when yesterday was all about the here and now
It's no surprise I find myself here right now

Though Pain and Sorrow are with me for the ride
They'll soon make more room for Anger and Fear
They never were the best of friends
But sometimes they're the only ones I have

To avoid this endless loop of self-pity
I have to become a better man

Yesterday, I joined the band of anonymity
Today, I accept this road is just for me

In order to avoid this endless loop
I have to become a better man
But I don't know if I want to
I don't know if I can

VI. RESOLVE

LOST
PART 2

How did I get here?
The part of me that I've been a part of
And has been a part of me for so long
Is now apart
Not because she died
But because she decided she'd rather die without me

The part of me
That I've tried so hard to please
Tried so hard to figure out
Constantly making me learn and grow along the way
Constantly putting me on the edge of my seat
Is gone

Now just an acquaintance with passing tolerance

So here I am
Not knowing who I am
Not knowing what all those years and effort was all about
I'm left with all the freedom
And all the limitations
I thought I'd never experience again

The easy thing to do

Is to find someone else to fill that gap
Danger! Willa Robinson!
There's a widower on the prowl!
That would be the easy thing to do, wouldn't it?
Fill the gap with someone else

Preferably someone who is the exact opposite of all the things
That I hated about you the whole time!

Maybe for all the wrong reasons
They're right
This is not what I need right now
To fill the holes
After all that damage that we created
Maybe that's not what I need

Because if that happened
Where would I end up?
The exact same place I'm at
7 to 8 years from now
Doing it all over again!
With feeling!

No thanks

I've learned
I'll never be happy
Through you
For you
With you
The thing we've done all these years?
It will never be enough

Because I was meant to go places
Meant to leap tall buildings in a single bound
I'm older now
And gray
But I still have time to do this
I still have some time

I'll start walking
Hand in hand with my kids
The only real things left to me in this world
I don't exactly how we'll get there
I don't know exactly how long it will take

But I know we'll get there

TREKKIES

It was always like this, wasn't it?
A race to the top
A fight for what was left
We contended for the hurt
The damaged and the lost
The beautiful and the damned

The plumes of smoke
From an ever-changing world drove us to extremes
Out of necessity, the smartest among us created a new world
They got rich and naked
While the rest of us were forced
To fend for ourselves

Scattered from the birth of the Wildfire

149

We fought hard just to survive
The more battles we fought
The more we lost
Until we realized conventional wisdom
No longer applied

We were squires in the joust
Against knights who made their rounds
Desired by those we loved and loved by them to exhaustion
They were the forbidden fruit, now accessible to all
The rules that we worked so hard to understand
No longer applied

This new reality
Pushed some to turn back and consign themselves
To solitude and the life of the destitute
We couldn't handle the new ways
With their endless defeats
And their constant rejections

For others,
There was the relief of the compromise
They settled in a settled land
Because that was the only option available
They learned to live with it
But they died every day because of it

A few
Seethed with resentment
And filled up their bitter wells
And endlessly played their violins

As they sent themselves and others
Straight into oblivion

For the smallest number among us
We saw only two choices
Be consumed
Or pave a trail
We weren't smart like the early pioneers
But we weren't ready to cede like the others

So we rolled up our sleeves
Defied the gods
And set out for distant seas
Not for ego
Not out of unwillingness to accept reality
But for our own sanity and survival

Because even though our world has changed
Our needs have not
We still fight for food and air
A place to call our own
Someone to call our home
A name that we can embrace

And we will do it
On our own terms
In our own way

Everything has changed
Everything remains the same

STAY

Reaching out to others
Always reaching out

Wherever he goes
Whatever he does

He's always reaching out to others

Until…One day…
A voice…

Stop
Stop reaching out

But if I don't reach out to others, he tells the voice,

Then no one will reach out to me.

Stop
Just stop reaching out

He wavers…
But the voice is firm

So, he stops
And he's right

No one does

So he sits
And he's alone

And he sits, and he's alone for a long, long time

It's so long
That he finds things to do
Just to keep himself busy

He finds things to do that he likes
And finds out about things that he doesn't like

He does things that build him up
That make him stronger
That make him wiser

That make him better

He keeps himself busy
And he changes

He keeps himself busy, and he changes for a long, long time

It's so long
That he doesn't notice
When someone reaches out for him

Then someone else

Soon, there are so many people reaching out for him
So many people asking for his attention
That he will never have to reach out to anyone ever again

But he doesn't reach out to them
Because he no longer cares

He's different now
He's changed

But he discovers
They're all still just the same

FEAR

At first, I thought I was just afraid for myself
Fear of loneliness
Fear of broken-heartedness
Desperately reaching for another
To get back what was lost

But the truth is less kind

I've been afraid for so much more
Because the truth is, my son and my daughter,
I failed you
I could not provide you the happy home you so richly deserved
I could not love your mother to the ends of the earth

I've failed

And I've been running from the truth ever since

I am desperate now, my children
I'm desperate to repair what I broke in your world
To give you what you what you need
I am so sorry
I am so sorry

I am so sorry

I did not do everything I could
I did not change fast enough
Was not willing enough
Refused to be strong enough
And you deserve better

You deserve better

But...

Your dad can change

I will pick us up from the ashes
We'll reach the highest peak
My prince and my princess
We'll get to our kingdom on the clouds
We'll get there

Your dad will change

I'm done now
I'm done feeling sorry for myself
I'm done chasing tails, done walking into dead-ends

I'm done thinking about all the things that went wrong
And I'm going to start focusing on all the things that are right

We're alive
We're together
We're healthy
We're going to make it
And we're going to continue making it all the way to the top

Because your dad
Just won't quit
He is figuring out this thing called life
And learning how to build this all on his own
Just like your grandfather did at one time

He got us on his rocket and took a leap to this land
A tremendous feat of strength
We broke all boundaries
We sought adventure!
You were fearless, Dad.

Somewhere along the way, things got lost
I don't know what did us in
But you took us as far as you could go
And I thank you, Dad.
I'll take us at least one step further

We're gonna do this, my children
We're gonna rise from the fucking ashes
We're gonna get out of this cardboard box
And have our hearts and our lives filled to the brim

157

We're gonna do this

And we're gonna get there together

ASSENT

Some truths
Cut too deep to express

The only choices you have

Are to bury them,
Let them bury you,

Or dig them up everyday
And expose them to the fire of your toil

ART OF WAR

Inch by inch
Word by word

This must be done the old-fashioned way

Take over the world
By blood, sweat, and destruction

BAPTISM BY FIRE

Every word I write
Burns off a little more of the weakness

ACCEPTANCE

Love is dead
There's nothing for me on the other side

I'm OK with this

MY QUOTAS

Gone are the days to take off or check out
To allow exceptions and say, "I deserve this!"
Every day it's just about getting better
Every day it's just about getting it done

Even though there will always be a better way of doing things
Even though I've always wanted perfection
It's time to just get it done
Stop talking. Just do it

DON'T EVER FORGET

Don't ever forget
That your kids are the most important to you
That your dreams are the most important to you
And that's all that matters

That's all that matters

So when you're working on either thing,
Be joyful
That's what life is all about
That's what's most important

Don't look back
Don't lean to the side
Look forward
Stay focused

And stay on track

The lives of those who veered off course
Are too numerous to count
The lives of those who stayed true
Are truly something to behold

Stay on track
Stay on track
Your children and your dreams
Stay on track

A GOOD RUN

It was a good run
Twenty years of my life
Seeking to save what was lost
Riding high as the holy roller
Though I wasn't perfect
And I would never be
That was OK
It's how you saw me

You helped me when I needed you
Gave me answers
Instilled discipline
Provided me a measure of solace
But even then
After all these years

I couldn't shake the feeling
That it was me who was still lost inside

Because it was never about me, was it?
It was always about your will, your purpose
Your way or the highway
Everything else was self-aggrandizing
Even as I was left fantasizing
About big cars, big homes, big dreams
And maybe just…
A little peace of mind

Regardless
Through it all
You taught me good things
You've kept me out of the darkest barrios
The creepy corners conjured within my own heart
The edifices envisioned from my worst fears
You kept me from the places I could go in my worst lows
And taught me how to endure the worst woes

It wasn't a perfect relationship
I never thought it would be
Good times, bland times, mad times,
Sometimes a waste of time
I met some great mentors, made some good friends
And got caught up
With some manipulative holier-than-thou fuckwads
Even your enemy couldn't defend

But in the end
I have no regrets
Even if I have nothing to show but these two angels in my life
That is more than enough for me
It's better than anything I could have ever imagined
More precious than I dared hope
Because they're the best thing that ever happened to me
They're the best thing that ever happened to me

But in the end
I need to go
I want to find my own happiness
Reach my own destiny
On my own terms
In my own way
I want to start
Listening to my heart over my head

Only you know how much I tried
And maybe through it all
Breaking free is just another lesson from you to me
But it was a good run
You know you'll always be a part of me
I hope I can be a part of you
Today, tomorrow,
And in the Day to come

MAN IN THE MIRROR

Here's the thing
You set your sights so high
But you work ethic is ehhh
You work, sure
But is it any good?

You say you don't want to punch clocks
You say you want to be king
You want your son and your daughter to be the prince and
princess
And go all the way to the top
But here's the thing

Who doesn't?

And her?
You want her to be your queen
Because being king will be the only way she'll accept you
Someone else?
Maybe a house and a 401K would be enough

So here you are
Sights set so high
Unwilling to live with anything less
Your dreams
Right now, they're nothing but a heavy burden

But they're also the only hope you have left

So you want to know how to get there?
Do you really want to know?
Then this is what you have to do
Switch on the focus, switch on the grind
Switch on the motherfuckin' beast

Just switch the fuck on

Train like the MMA fighters
Live a boring life of routine, repetition, and resilience
Every bite, every punch, every ounce of output
Needs to be measured, monitored, and maxed out
Everything needs be maxed out

This is your time
This is your only time
This will require something extraordinary

There ain't nothing casual or pleasant about this, son
You must enter into hell willingly and kill all fear

Train
Train with the best
Get help from those who are better
Tune out the world
Tune out all those who aren't doing and will never get it done

Get into the zone
Go narrow-minded
Turn on the tunnel vision
Until all you see are your goals ahead
And your children next to you

Nothing else matters. Nothing

Build your vessel
Eat clean. Silly rabbit, desserts are for kids
Train for strength
No drinking. You want vino or primo?
Lose the weight, build the strength

Just do it

Write
Lock the doors
Your kitchen table is your training ground
Your pen is your gloves, your paper is the punching bag
Don't stop until you're done

Money
Stop spending
Budget, track, and invest
Don't look for girls
You got dreams to focus on, bitch

You want this?
Then do it
There is no more wanting
Be the king that you are
Go get that fucking life

ABUNDANCE

It's time
To stop thinking about all the things that I don't have
And all the things that might have been
It's time to say goodbye to all that

I'm ready
To focus on all the good things that will be coming my way
And all the great things I already have
I'm ready to start focusing on all that

Like my two children, my son and my daughter
And the love that we share as a family

Like our health and well-being
And the fact that we have it

Like the home that we live in
And the safety that we live under

Like the money and prosperity that we have
And the floodgates of wealth that will be pouring in

Like the dreams we are fulfilling
And the strength we have in our bodies and our minds to fulfill
them

I'm ready to turn over to this new chapter
Let the good times come in
Let's the good times keep coming in

THE KEY

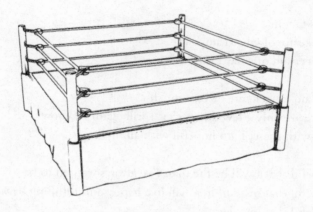

You want success?
Harness the pain

Choose your harness wisely
And bring on the pain

ANCHORS

I was taught
To be sure of what I hope for
And certain of what I do not see

I am no longer sure of very much
There are only a few things that I still claim to know
And with these, I am hopeful with all my heart

Hopeful that I will be the man I've always wanted to be
Hopeful that my children will live happy and fulfilling lives
Hopeful that one day…

You will find your way to me

While this world provides no certainties
Of this I am sure
My hopes remain my absolute

QUESTIONS

Why?
Why can't I get out of bed?
Why do I keep feeling this way?
Am I an addict?
Am I lazy?

Am I undisciplined?
Should I have another handful of chips?
Why don't I have more goddamn likes?
Are my pills not working?
Can't I just follow the plan?

Do I really look like that?
Why are some blessed and other cursed?
Does positive affirmation work?

Why can't I focus?
I wonder if I have any ice cream left in the fridge

Every day requires hard choices
Every day requires the same choices
Just follow the plan
Get out of bed
And just follow the plan

VISUALIZATION

All I see in my head
Is the Amazon counter breaking records
As the number of people reading my books
Goes from 1 to 100,000,000

All I see in my head
Is making a fortune
Quitting my job
Going on the talk-show circuit
Karaoking Jay Z on Jimmy Fallon
Enjoying the fruits of being an "overnight" sensation

And then I see
My story being picked up by HBO
A 30-minute drama
Based on my true story of living and dating
As a 40-year-old Asian man with two kids in the 21st century
All the struggles
All the nights
Writing poems on my iPhone
After coming home alone

Maybe the last part needs some work…

NARA

Lamps dimly lit
Setting carefully crafted
Oak furnishings, copper finish fixtures
Reminiscent of a colonial empire risen and now only
remembered

Finely mixed drinks
From ingredients all around the world
Endless possibilities
Limited only by the desire of the requester

This is art

Seen through a glass
Tasted through the lips
Permeating into the soul
Awakening the mind

A blend of so many flavors
So complex
Yet the taste so clean
So pure

This is art
Inspiration from the other side of the world

In here, nothing is accidental
Even the artist's thin frame
Is less nature and more a lifetime of refrain
Built not on excess but to dedication

May I rise up to the challenge
Of living a life as focused as this

Of making art as pure as this

ONE PATH

Put to rest
Your burning desires
That consume and dishearten,
And awaken
Your inciting fires
That revive and enlighten

All roads lead to the same destination
If you stay on the road of your current motivations
But the path leading to your joyous terminal
There's really only one

If you take that singular trail,
All the schemas and paradigms
All the constructs and archetypes

182

That seek to define you
Will be forever changed
And fall in your favor

MOTIVES

It's not the comfort I seek anymore

It's the truth of my voice
The integrity of my actions
And the blood from my toil

I'M COMING

I see you now
So clearly

Even though you were always there
Scratching me from the corners of my brain
Wrenching me from my insides

Teasing me to come closer
Making my head spin with your primrose promises
Inviting me in for drinks

Then pulling away
Leaving me to satiate myself
In any way I could

Just so I could deny you really existed

I tried to convince myself it was about anything but you
About Her, About God, About Inner Peace
But none of those things could dull the calling I had for you

But I know now I was wrong
It was about you
It was always about you

And I want you to know...
I'm coming

With the same amount of effort I put toward begging her,
begging God
I'm going to use that fixation to find you
And I am going to find you

And when I do
I'm not going to take you aside
For pleasantries and puff pastries

I'm not going to embrace you
As if we were some long-lost friends
Or soulmates finding each other before the closing credits

No
Not like that

I'm gonna headshot you with my 12-gauge
And dunk over your ass like Michael Jordan on Game 7 of the
Finals
And Mike Tyson knock you out

I'm going to hunt you down in the wilderness
And bearclaw your guts out
And leave your remains for the jackals

I don't want a seat at the table anymore
I want the whole fucking table
And all the beautiful silverware that goes with it

Then I'm going to buy the building where the table resides
Renovate and refurbish it
And then burn it all down

And then I'm gonna build it back up the way that I want it
The way that it was always meant to be
And I'm going to laugh at your gravestone when it's complete

Because you were always there
Eluding me
Mocking me
Scratching me from the corners of my brain
Wrenching me from my insides

This was never about love
It wasn't about diversions in Cancun or business class flights to
Singapore
This was about you

It was about finding you
And conquering you
It was all about conquering you

The great adversary
My great destiny

I'm coming

SLIVER

There is wealth beyond measure
Abundance beyond belief
Infinite possibilities
Limitless opportunities
The prospects are endless
The resources abound
...for some

80% of the world
Want to be loved by the 20%
While the 20%
Long to be with the 4
A world of endless fractals
But none of it matters
When you're the poorest of the poor

They say stay positive
Keep a healthy mindset
Fill up with optimism and affirmations
Mantras and meditations
I say…
Fuck you

We're swimming against the tide
Defying all the odds
Going against the grain
And kicking against the goads
There's nothing positive and peaceful about this
Nothing remotely kind

It's brutal and it's violent
It's cruel and it's merciless
If it's transcendence and nirvana we desire
It's affliction and pain we must face
There will be blood
Because this is war

Like a filthy peasant
I fight the warlords of this world
With nothing but a pitchfork and a sling
Against cannons and muskets
Armies and armories
A lone man with a lone cause

Against these odds, I will die
I'll die by arrow
I'll die by spear
I'll die by machine guns and in open fire

I'll die even before I reach the first wave
I'll die in every way imaginable

But no matter how many times I die
I'll be back
Like a poor man's T-800
Like an Asian Phil on Groundhog Day
I'll be back
Back to pitch a fork straight up your ass
And send you straight down to hell

Because there is love and there is war
And there's nothing in between
Not for those on the bottom
Not for people like us
We wake up every morning
To break every existing barrier

MONDAY NIGHT

Kids are in bed
Fed, showered, and brushed
I'm tired
I have three more emails to send
And one hour to write

Write about what?
I don't know. Just keep going
I'm tired
No one cares
Keep going
Keep going

THE SUM OF ALL THINGS

When I go all out
Pushing myself to the max
Gasping for air, clinging to my knees
I realize it's only when I'm here
That I know what I'm made of

The quality of what I put in yesterday
Determines the distance I can run today
It's humbling to know
It doesn't get me very far
I've let myself go for too long

But as much as it hurts to do it
I have to look at the scoreboard
Only by running as a sloth

And pitting myself against the gazelles
Do I realize how much I need to change

The late-night drinking
The Netflix binges
Overspending, overcommitting
Winding down, tuning out
Proselytizing
Chasing tails
They all add up
To going nowhere

It's time, you and I,
To cast off everything that hinders
And all the momentary pleasures that so easily entangle
And run the race marked out for us
Work. Prepare. Work again

Run as if your life and dreams depend on it
Because they do
Every decision counts
Every moment matters
It's just you and me, my friend,
We'll get there in the end

ICARUS

The story of Icarus is poison
Keep your children away!
A story of a boy who dared to fly so high
Only to come crashing down
Because he refused to stay in his pre-labeled space
His death a warning tale
To all those who should dare to be so bold

Perhaps in today's illiterate
But technologically advanced society
The one benefit we can claim
Is that we're too connected
To listen to the cowards of the past
Who remind us not to sail over the edge
Who assure us that Babel was for our benefit
And order us to bow to the phony monarchs of our lands

Icarus was born to fly
So let him fly
Let him go high and far, out to the great beyond
Let him aspire to achieve the highest dream
Let him defy the limits of our preconceived notions
As well as the laws of space and time
To help us get to where we all need to go

MORNING ROUTINE

Grind the coffee
Grind out the words
And shut the fuck up

TRUDGE

Some days are great
Free-flowing
Effortless and easy
And the stars are in alignment

Most days
A trudge
A grind
A fight just to stay awake

Most days
A trudge

IT'S HAPPENING

I'm just beginning my journey
But I'm beginning to feel the change
By constantly writing out my thoughts
True, authentic, and unapologetic
And saturating myself with visuals and reminders
Of what I want and what I'm working for
I'm beginning to see life take a new direction

Over the last several months, I'm beginning to see who I can
become
Not a person defined by circumstance
But one who can define the circumstances
By working incessantly on my life's calling
And not just responding to the calls of others
By pursuing my goals
My heart and my spirit are changing

I could not be grateful then
Even if I tried
And that's assuming I even wanted to
But now it's possible to fathom the words "thank you"
"You're welcome" and "please"
It's possible to even say this
Without saying, "Give me a fucking break"

It's possible
It's happening
I'm coming
In a quantum dimension,
I'm already there

TENRI

A temple
With hallways of glistening wood
Oceans of impeccably aligned tatami
Immaculate, orderly, beautiful

If my insides can match my outside
And my outside could be sculpted new
I want both to be like this
Peaceful, pristine, perfect

In all the corners of the world
Of all the monuments I've seen
This one is best
This one... deeply moves

What inspires such devotion
To keep this construct
Without spot or blemish?
What inspires such devotion?

To create order that produces calm?
To create tidiness that evokes divinity?
Not by accident
Nor by alignment of stars

Not from forced labor
Demanded by cruel and charismatic overseers
But through voluntary devotion
Through choice and callused knees

Let my faults and my mental chaos
My anger and my arrogance
Be swept away like dust from ritual cleaning
Like them be swept away like dust

In this moment
I'm delivered the answers I already know
To reach the peace I so earnestly seek
And in this moment, I accept

I'm given an able body
A sound enough mind
And a longing soul
All of them I accept with joy

Now I must practice the daily diligence
To sweep away the faults of my past
Work diligently on my knees
And connect with the perfection of the divine

TO DO

Wake up
Love your kids
Read
Write
Eat
Work
Exercise
Sleep

Wake up
Love your kids
Read
Write…

I AM

Who am I?
In this time and in this place?
Just writhing tentacles of emotions and desires
Conflicting yearnings for love and space?

Sitting alone on many nights, I've wondered
What have I accomplished?
Where exactly have I been?
And where, pray tell, am I going?

How many times have I failed?
How many more times am I going to fail?
How much time do I have I left?
Is there anything left I have within me?

Is my chance for greatness gone?
Did I even have a chance?
Is this my lot in life?
Do I just grin and bear it from here?

What am I going to do?

What am I going to do?

What am I going to do?

If I can start
By letting go of my fears and doubts
By refusing to define myself by anyone else's terms but my own
Maybe I can find out

Maybe I can find out

So I start
By writing out these words and planning out my goals
And attaching them to impossible dates
And connecting them to impossible numbers

And I can start to tell you who I am

I can tell you who I am
And I'll tell you who I motherfucking am

I am the Great Architect
Building empires within my mind
One day those empires will be a physical reality
With every brick I lay, with every word I write

I am the Devoted Father
To my son and to my daughter
Because of them I never look back
When today is filled with such joy and laughter

I am the Fearsome Destroyer
Nothing can keep me down
I overcome fear and illness, weakness and calamity
I choke out the Great Adversary, and he begs for my mercy

I am the Achiever of Dreams
When Doubt laughs at my lofty goals, I slap her ugly face
Because nothing is outside my reach
I will always attain; I will always gain

I am the Alpha and the Omega
Though a Higher Power there may be,
When it comes to the outcomes of my life,
It begins and ends with me

I don't pray for rain
I am the Rainmaker

All this and more, I am
I am what I am
And I am the Great I Am

THAT WAS THEN,
THIS IS NOW

My eyes open
It's morning
I check the calendar to see what I have planned for the day
And realize
It's my birthday

And I'm all alone

There was a time
When that realization would have scared me
Or saddened me
Or driven me to something else—anything else
Just to take it all away

But that was then
And this is now

Now I am building my empire
Burning away the sludge
Defying time and space
The mountaintop that awaits
Is already here in my mind

Coulda shoulda woulda
Are all things in the past
I'm moving, I'm pushing, I'm changing
But it's time to take a brief pause
It's time to recalibrate

The focus and the effort
Have been good
But the championship match is closing in
I'll need to dial it up
I'll need to dial it the fuck up

The doors are locked
The computer is revved
All I see is this narrow window
All I have is this narrow window
To focus like I never have before

On this day
I give to myself
The present of no excuses
The present of no lies and no remorse
Happy birthday to me

Time to get what's mine

A TOAST

Let us toast today
For the harvest to come tomorrow
From the labors of yesterday

VII. VISION

LESSON OF LOVE

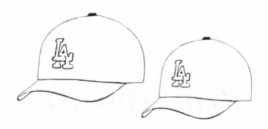

My son,
If the girl you love says goodbye
Let her go
If she is quick to point out your faults
Or threatens to leave because of them
Let her leave

Give your heart fully
And be the man that you aspire to be
For yourself
For your calling
If you change, do it for yourself
Not to appease someone else

If you find yourself trying to break down her walls
They won't

Or think she'll change in time
She won't
If you think in time she'll come around
She never will

When you're ready to give your heart fully to her without fear
You'll know
When she gives her heart fully to you without looking back
You'll know
Because it won't be some problem to figure out
Or some mystery to be explored

It will be because you gave it your best
During all the times you weren't with her
And she gave it her best
During all the times she wasn't with you
Love is not too halves making a whole
Your individual completeness will draw you together

If I can be as strong in my life as these words suggest
Perhaps there is hope for me as well
To lead and guide you
Not just with my words, but with my life
This is what I commit to you
From this day forward

THE WAY IT'S GOING TO BE

Hey
Thank you for agreeing to meet me
It's been a long time

I know you were wondering why I called you
After the way things ended
And all the years that have passed
There's something that I need to tell you
And thank you in advance for listening

When last you heard from me
Maybe the only time you've heard from me
I spoke with the voice of correction
With commands and commandments
With warnings and disapprovals

I understand why you don't reach out to me anymore

I'm sorry

I've been doing a lot of thinking
Soul searching and self-inventorying
I've been considering all that I've done
All that I'm capable of doing
And all those I can hurt if I'm not careful with who I am

After all that we've been through
I've never taken the time to tell you
All the good things about you
All the things you're doing right
I've never told how much I value you
And how highly I think of you

And I'm sorry

Things will be different
Because I will be different
Because I will choose to be different

I know you've been through some rough times
I know you feel like you've lost so much and gained so little
I know you blame yourself for all of it

But I'm here to tell you
As hard as it is
As hard as it can continue to be

Life is still good
And your life will turn out great

Because you're great
And because I believe in you

I know that sometimes you hate the world for how it can be
Sometimes you hate yourself for how you are
You wish you could be better
You wish you wouldn't make the same mistakes over and over
again
You wish you could be a better father to your kids
You wish you could provide more for them

But I'm here to tell you
There is still magnificence in this world
You're a magnificent person
And everyday you're choosing to get better and better
Even though you're already great
Everyday you're getting stronger and stronger
Even though you're already strong

And your kids?
Well, your kids think you're pretty fucking awesome

You'll get to where you want to go
You know it as well as I do
But don't forget to enjoy the journey along the way
The place that you call a box
Is still home to you and your kids
Continue to nurture it and tend to it

Love and appreciate it
Before bigger things come,
And bigger things will come,
Learn to value the things that are here today

Don't get down on yourself for pursuing love
After all, what is more important in life?
Just understand it's not just about what you're willing to give
It's what you allow yourself to accept
And I want you to accept only the best
I want you to accept only the best

You're pursuing your passion
You're working your dreams
You're making each day memorable
You're making each day count

I'm proud of you

Laugh as much as you can
Pause to take in the beauty and the privilege of life
Be a great friend to your friends
Plant and tend to your wealth
Believe me, you'll have a lot more coming soon

Most importantly
Above all else
Remember this…

The only opinions that matter in this life
Are of those who think about you all the time

Your kids
And me

After all, I'm here with you until the end
And I think you're pretty fucking awesome too

HOPE

I hope you find someone who makes you laugh
Who makes your heart skip a beat
And treats you with all the kindness and the love that you
deserve

I hope on your journey to finding him
You find peace and joy within yourself
And the purpose and the life that you have always dreamed of

I hope you learn to sing again
Like you did when you were five on your grandmother's
recorder
Singing with eagerness and abandon

I hope you learn to play the piano
Not for him or for those in the pew
But out of the sheer desire to create something beautiful for
yourself

I hope you make the difference
And create the change that you seek
I hope everyone listens and that everyone learns

I hope to walk you down the aisle
And send you off to the man whom you will love
And who will love you with all his heart and with every
definition of goodness

And you laughed
You laughed in disbelief
When I said I wanted to be there for your wedding day

But I hope that he will love you more than I could
And be stronger and gentler to you in ways that I could not
I hope that you have a bright and happy future together

And no matter how things have turned out
These years with you were the best of my life
I wish you all the best in the many years ahead

SORRY, NO

Yeah, that didn't turn out so well
Pouring my heart out to you
Like a broken dam
So unexpectedly and suddenly
After all these years

Sorry, no
Was your response
Been too long
There's still him
We're just getting to know each other again

Sure, okay
Was my response
We can just be friends
Great ones!
Life goes on

But here's the thing...
I know something you don't

We didn't come this far
Experiencing what we have
Losing what we lost
Wanting what we do
For us to be apart

Sure, okay, I'll shut my heart down
And work to pick myself back up
I'll be the person I want to be
And somewhere along the way
You'll see exactly as I do

That we were meant to be

So, sorry, no
I'm not going to give up
I will always have hope
Because the stars will one day align in our favor
Or I will rewrite the stars to make it so

DUST IN THE WIND

What was once so important in the beginning
The chasing of this world
The groping of our desires
Will burn away like chaff in the end

The torrents of fear and angst
That mark the halls of our generation
Are the familiar fruits we have reaped
Hidden behind our social media photos from Ibiza

This is the game I've let define me
But this is the game I no longer want to play
These are the rules I no longer want to live by
I want to walk far, far away

Because they are all dust in the wind

I want to discover my own truths
And be resolute in knowing what I stand for
Let me write them down on paper
And remind myself of them daily

And as I hold to my truths every day
I'll watch as my whims and my whines weaken
And the pulsing in my head will subside
As peace and clarity settle in

May I fight to live this way until the end
May I work toward my dreams until I succeed
Let me not measure myself by what I want you to see
But only who I've proven to myself to be

But in the end, this too, shall be dust in the wind

I want my children and their children beside me
My legacy and love filled to the brim and passed over
Everything that I worked for, everything I lived for
Standing beside me when I die

Even if there is nothing on the other side
Even if I'm told I went the wrong way
I'll know that I have lived
I'll know that it was right for me

And I'm good with that

TO ALL THE DATES
I'VE HAD BEFORE

I came into this
Hoping to get something out of this
And if I'm totally honest with myself
I wasn't totally honest with you

Yeah, there are a lot of guys out there
Who just want one thing from you
And as much as I hated them for creating walls within you
The truth of the matter is

I wasn't any different

I was going through pain and process
And wanted you to just make it go away
I was focused on taking and conquering
Rather than understanding and investing

You're going through a journey all your own
In this new age of the Wildfire
The pressures are immense for you
And the clock is shorter for you

It's a whole new world

I don't understand what you're going through
And as much as I'd like to say I'll never understand
I'm not going to say that
I'm going to say I'm going to really try

We're all in this together
I'm sorry for the pains that you've gone through
When men like me said they were ready for you
But they weren't ready for you at all

Many of us would never be ready

So instead of "fuck off" and "whatever"
Instead of "she's just a narrow-minded, aging woman"
And all the other bad thoughts I've thought in the past
As a result of my bruised ego, my insecurities, and my selfish
interests

Let me just start by saying I'm sorry
I'm sorry for misrepresenting who I am
And thank you
Thank you for closing the door on me

So that I could learn to open it for myself

THE STRANGER

I invested so much in doing what is right
That I forgot to do what is right for me
And now I'm caught in the in-between
Having nothing to my name
Except a clear conscience
and a single-digit bank account

I refuse to look back and think of all the time that was lost
But I'm afraid to look ahead toward the dreams I've never built

I wander as a stranger in this world
Surrounded by the street-wise and the world-weary
Surprised by customs of love and friendship I've never known
Surrendered to the distances that make other people
comfortable

I will work as a stranger in this new world
To bring a gift only I can give
And find those who are lost like me
For I seek not to change myself into its image
But to change it into mine

FIND YOU

Somewhere along this journey I will find you
Preferably sooner than later
But likely
Not for a long time

When we meet
I will be tired but accomplished
I will have gotten to the places where I have set my mind to go
And reaped the fruits from what I set my hands to sow

The doubts will have melted away
The fears will have dissolved
And the patience that was required
Will no longer ask me to wait another day

And even though we have never met
We'll have gotten to know each other very well by then

Every hour spent chiseling away at the slate
Will narrow the distance between us

Your hands will be steady from the pain endured
Your voice will be calm
And hopefully your heart will still be warm
Rather than callused from the many years of war

We'll make a toast you and I
With the finest whiskey that money can buy
You'll be a better version of me
When I find you in the day to come

4TH OF JULY

We are living better than we ever have
Never having experienced the semblance of war
Nor fearing it for our children
Hell and its aftermath is the reality our forefathers died to
extinguish

I have good food to eat
I am in good health and in moderately good spirits
I have no fears of a deadly outbreak
And have access to medicines that can cure almost any disease

I'm living in a good time, perhaps the best time
I can create the stories that are in my head
And no matter how vivid the conspiracies are
I have the comfort and safety to write them

There is still violence and hatred
There is still centuries-long narrowmindedness
Corruption, manipulation, and greed are rampant
There are still so many in need

But we are better and stronger
Than we were yesterday
We can be good, not just to each other
But to ourselves

And we will get better

America, we are beautiful

SOMEWHERE

There is a place

For those who speak a language of truth
A language without fear or compromise
Without bravado or deceit
But with vulnerability and clarity

For those who live by their own truths
But know that other truths exist
They admit they don't know everything
And are always open to listen and change if needed

There is a place

Where people can put down their masks
And burn them without eulogy
Where people tired from running
Can finally rest in their own selves

Where people live
Not for profits and plunder
Not for exploitation and erosion
But for self-worth and mutual betterment

Where people treat each other
With respect and consideration

Who see through the eyes of unadulterated self-awareness
And seek to heal and not to harm

There is a place

Where people, acknowledging the ways of this world,
Are able to defend their beliefs with a sword
But only to protect those they love
And to defend the ideals that keep them together

Where the appointed leaders will not be free from error
But they will be free from corruption
They know that the laws of the land and the spirit of the
people
Will always be their first and only duty

This place calls for men and women to be brave
To stand together and to fight
Against the forces of darkness
The corrupt, the defilers, the greedy

To fight those dark forces that protect only what is theirs
Motivated by the illusion that there is never enough for
everyone
These monsters will do everything they can
To ensure everyone never has enough

The brave men and women of this new world need to do
whatever it takes
To protect their ideals
To change and grow with the passage of time
And prepare the roads for others to follow

I am convinced that such a place can exist
Not in theory or in imagination
Not in limited scale or short duration
But for here, for everyone, and for all eternity

Let us build this place
You and I
And work and rest and fight and love there
For you and me and all our children

THE HANDS OF TIME

Many of those who make it to the top
Will become just like the forefathers they've hated
Another cog in the infinite machine of destruction
Vilifying the world for the hurt they've endured

But there will be a few
Who will climb up, look back, reach out, and say,
"I've forgiven others, please forgive me
And let's light up the world."

I hope you and I can be the latter

TRAVERSE

There are terrains
Too difficult to cross
When it is time to finally set forth
We find any reason to turn back

There are truths
Too difficult to accept
When the flashback hits
We do anything to push it back

There are tragedies
Too difficult to cope
After they strike
We resign ourselves to the coming apocalypse

But after you've run out of excuses
And people to blame and to hate

After you've pulled bare the beer and wine shelves
And you've refused the naked arms of others

After you have endured the endless storm
After you've accepted
After you've processed
And you've grieved

Let's go back to that terrain
And let's cross that motherfucker

THE PURPLE ROOM

I take a moment
And step away from the busy kitchen
To walk through the hall with ambient lights
Of purple pendants casting purple hues
And go to the end of the corridor
Where I reach the golden door

Even before I turn the knob, I can already hear
Music and laughter coming from the other side
The sounds of celebration
The sounds of happiness
Not to commemorate my end
But only the end of my beginning

I open the door to see the faces of those whom I love
All my invited guests, my family and my friends
They're here to rejoice with me
For finally putting all my words to pages
And sending out the sum of the pages
For all the world to see

Like every creator before me and after
I wait with bated breath during the moment of release
Knowing that this is the moment when anything is possible
When mountains can be moved, fortunes can be won
When hearts can be stirred

And lives can be changed forever

My children,
our lives will be changed forever

But the truth is, I don't know what tomorrow will bring
I know what the odds are
I know all about the chances, the likelihoods, and the
probabilities
But that's a world I refuse to accept
Not anymore, not ever
And certainly not tonight

Tonight is a time to celebrate
To toast the victory of possibility
The hope that only accomplishment can bring
While the response to these words is no longer under my
control
I can control what I do in this moment
And I choose to live tonight

I choose to give gratitude to my loved ones
To thank my children who are by my side
I want them to see their dad in this radiant light
An image imprinted in their minds
To pull it from their wallet
When times get tough

We'll have good food and drink
And pass the time with laughter and fun
It's mostly six degrees of separation

But the night will end with warm exchanges
We all have dreams
And the desire to fulfill those dreams gives us something in
common

I'd be remiss to say I didn't notice you
Wearing a red dress tonight
A color that you rarely wear
I know we're just friends for now
But maybe tonight, I moved the needle
Just a little

I take a moment
And step back into my busy kitchen
Where I go on writing these words today
Creating for all that will come tomorrow

One day, when you and I are in the purple room
I'll look back on what I wrote yesterday
When what was once considered tomorrow
Will be called tonight

WHEN

In the kitchen
With mahogany floors

In my home
With the ocean view

Built on a foundation of steel
and promises fulfilled

Coffee with you
As we watch our healthy and happy kids

That's when I'll know I've made it
That's when I'll know I'll be happy

Only then will I be happy

WHEN
PART 2

~~In the kitchen~~
~~With mahogany floors~~

~~In my home~~
~~With the ocean view~~

~~Built on a foundation of steel~~
~~and promises fulfilled~~

~~Coffee with you~~
~~As we watch our healthy and happy kids~~ My healthy and
happy children

~~That's when I'll know I've made it~~
~~That's when I'll know I'll be happy~~

~~Only then will I be happy~~

We will get there

ABOUT THE AUTHOR

Terry Kang is the father of two children. He's well on his way to finding himself.

To be added to my mailing list, please email me at tkanger1@gmail.com

Made in the USA
Coppell, TX
03 May 2021

54930890R00146